GREETINGS from ROUTE 66

Patrick, Michael, and Matthew Dahl

Rigby®

A Harcourt Achieve Imprint

www.Rigby.com
1-800-531-5015

Rt. 66 is one of the most famous roads in America. Built in 1926, it is more than 2,000 miles long.

Chicago
IL
Springfield
MO
St. Louis
Stanton
KS
Baxter Springs
CA
Barstow
Grand Canyon National Park
Catoosa
Claremore
Santa Monica
Kingman
Adrian
Amarillo
OK
Albuquerque
AZ
NM
TX

BARSTOW, CA

SANTA MONICA, CA

We saw this plaque at the beginning of our trip.

WILL ROGERS HIGHWAY
DEDICATED 1952
TO
WILL ROGERS
HUMORIST · WORLD TRAVELER · GOOD NEIGHBOR
THIS MAIN STREET OF AMERICA
HIGHWAY 66
WAS THE FIRST ROAD HE TRAVELED IN
A CAREER THAT LED HIM STRAIGHT TO
THE HEARTS OF HIS COUNTRYMEN

Dear Mom,

We left Santa Monica today. Dad is excited about driving the RV. He's already telling us stories about his trip on Rt. 66 when he was a kid. Rt. 66 was the Main Street of America. It goes through eight states. We'll drive through California, Arizona, New Mexico, Texas, Oklahoma, Kansas, Missouri, and Illinois. See you in two weeks.

Love, The Boys

Mrs.
Prude
Chicag
60601

This will be our home for 12 days.

day two
US
66

California state flower:
Golden Poppy

Driving to Arizona, we saw mountains in the distance.

AMBOY, CA

The road goes on
and on and on.

Dear Mom,

It's been a long day of driving. We stopped in the tiniest town—Amboy, California. Only 20 people live there. It's fun to think we added four more people when we drove through town. I liked when we drove through the Mojave Desert. We spotted lots of lizards, rattlesnakes, and cactus. We also saw hundreds of mice running across the road at night.

Love, Mike

Mrs.
Prud
Chic
606

We passed a ghost town along the way.

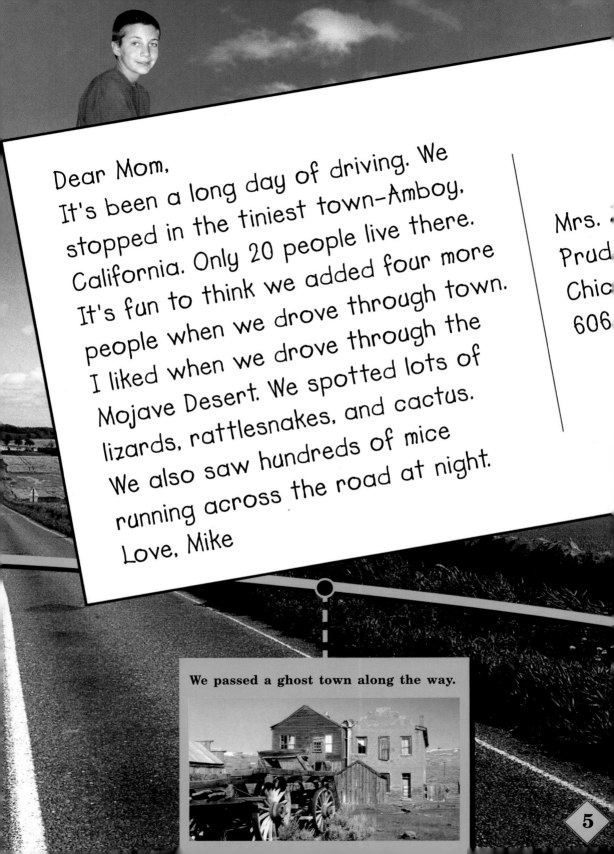

We almost took a helicopter ride over the Grand
Canyon, but Dad chickened out.

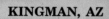

KINGMAN, AZ

Arizona state flower:
Saguaro (giant cactus)

Dear Mom,
  We saw the Grand Canyon and it's amazing! We couldn't stop looking at it! We all sat on the South Rim and watched the sun go down. This morning we met Angel and Juan Delgadillo. Juan owns a drive-in. He serves "hamburgers without ham" and "cheeseburgers with cheese." He was very funny. Angel owns a barbershop. We all watched Dad get a shave. Boy, did he need one.
Love, Pat

M
Pr
Ch
60€

Mr. Delgadillo sits in his shop.

Hubcap house

ALBUQUERQUE, NM

What a time for the air conditioner to break!

700 MILES
WATER
BAGS
THERMOS JUGS

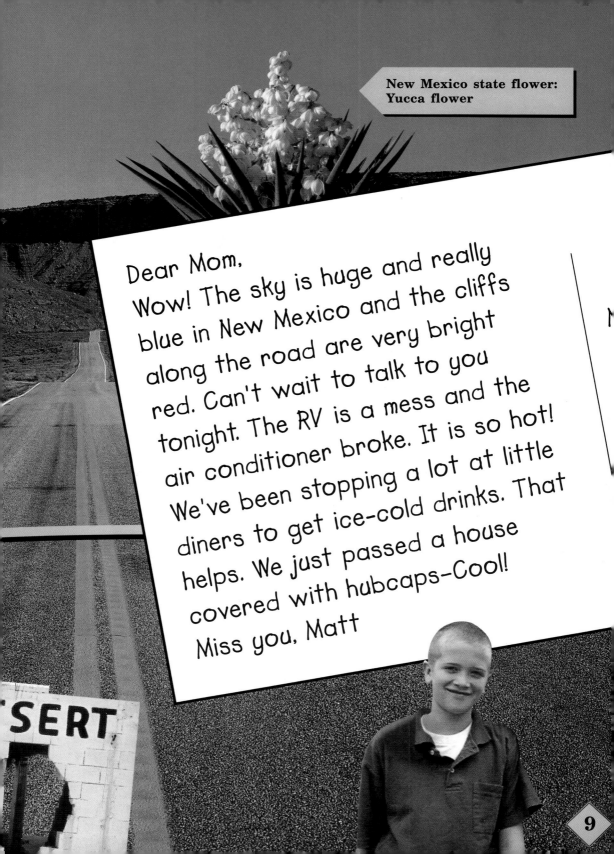

New Mexico state flower:
Yucca flower

Dear Mom,
Wow! The sky is huge and really blue in New Mexico and the cliffs along the road are very bright red. Can't wait to talk to you tonight. The RV is a mess and the air conditioner broke. It is so hot! We've been stopping a lot at little diners to get ice-cold drinks. That helps. We just passed a house covered with hubcaps-Cool!
Miss you, Matt

day five

U S 66

Dad stands at the halfway point.

MID POINT

WELCOME 66 ADRIAN,TX

ADRIAN, TX

Many ranchers raise Texas longhorns.

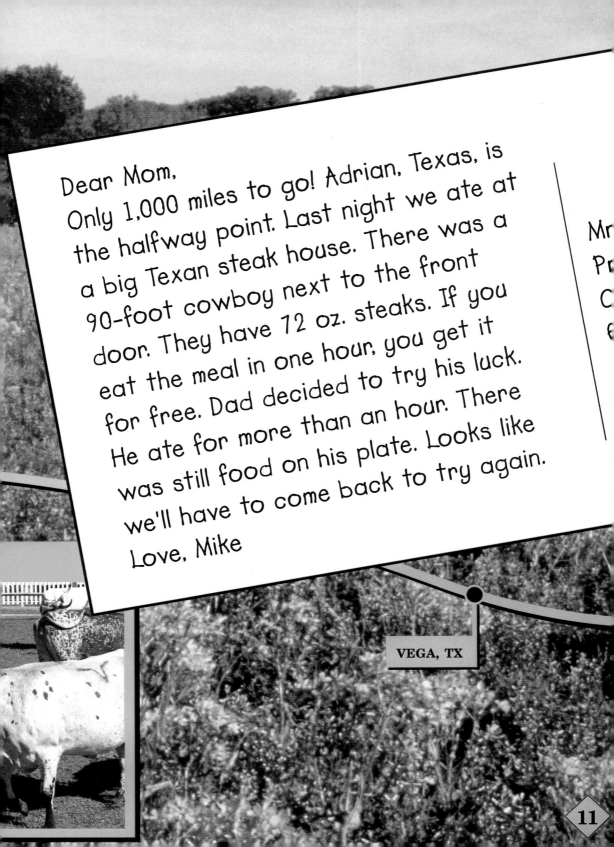

Dear Mom,

Only 1,000 miles to go! Adrian, Texas, is the halfway point. Last night we ate at a big Texan steak house. There was a 90-foot cowboy next to the front door. They have 72 oz. steaks. If you eat the meal in one hour, you get it for free. Dad decided to try his luck. He ate for more than an hour. There was still food on his plate. Looks like we'll have to come back to try again.

Love, Mike

Mr
Pi
C
6

VEGA, TX

day six

US 66

Windmills were everywhere!

Look at these cars sticking up out of the ground!

AMARILLO, TX

Texas state flower:
Bluebonnet

Dear Mom,

What a sight! There are ten BIG old cars buried in the middle of this wheat field in Amarillo, Texas. You can only see half of each of them. It's really wild. Dad said the cars were built from 1948 to 1964. Over the years, people have written their names on the cars with spray paint. We decided not to. Wow!

See you soon, Pat

Texas STATE LINE

The Will Rogers Memorial is in Claremore, OK.

CATOOSA, OK

Will Rogers

Dear Mom,
We got lost a lot today. The RV needs big spaces to turn! We found a swimming hole with a blue whale slide in Catoosa, Oklahoma. Dad made a huge splash when he slid into the water. Later we stopped at the Will Rogers Memorial. What a cool guy. He was a writer, an actor, and a cowboy. We might see a Will Rogers movie tonight. Dad's going to show us how to use a lasso after the movie!
Miss you, Mike

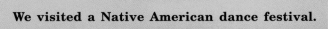

We visited a Native American dance festival.

day eight

US 66

Stretches of Rt. 66 are very narrow.

BAXTER SPRINGS, KS

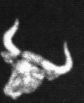

HOWDY, FRIEND
YOU'RE ENTERING
BAXTER SPRINGS
FIRST COW TOWN IN KANSAS

FOUNDED 1858   CHAMBER OF COMMERCE   POP. 5,000

16

Dear Mom,

Pat has been driving us crazy, but Dad made him promise not to tease and boss us around anymore. The part of the highway we are on is really narrow. We're about to cross from Kansas into Missouri. It took us no time to drive through Kansas. Only twelve miles of Rt. 66 are in Kansas. Dad will be happy to get through a state in one day. See you soon, Matt & Mike

Mrs. Jo
Pruden
Chicago
60601

Kansas state flower:
Sunflower

17

A small house fits inside the caverns!

MERAMEC CAVERNS
JESSE JAMES HIDEOUT

LES DILL   MERAMEC CAVERNS
ON HY. 66 STANTON, MO.

Frank and Jesse James.

Missouri state flower:
Hawthorn

Dear Mom,
You'd love Meramec Caverns in Missouri. They are underground paths that a man named Lester Dill discovered. The outlaw Jesse James and his gang used the caverns as a hideout back in the 1870s. There are lots of places to get lost here. Matt and Mike kept finding places to hide from Dad. He didn't think that was funny.
Love, Pat

Mrs
Pruc
Chico
6060

day ten
US 66

There were many tempting choices!

		Pineapple, bananas, coconut, and macadamia nut...	
Peach	Jim White	**Concrete:** 3.60	2.80
Butterscotch	Tart Cherry	Sundae: 3.20	
Whopper	Pralines		

CONCRETES

LARGE	3.40	
REGULAR	2.40	
MINI	1.60	

BANANA SPLIT- Three scoops of frozen c... topped with hot fudge, strawberries, pineapple w... and pecans.

DOTTIE- A concrete or sundae with mint, choco... macadamia nuts.

Concrete:	4.60	3.60
Sundae:	3.40	3.20

MALTS & SHAKES

LARGE	3.40	
REGULAR	2.40	

ALL SHOOK UP CONCRETE- ... of peanut butter cookie and bananas.

Concrete:	3.90	2.90

STRAWBERRY SHORTCAKE- topped with custard, strawberries and whipped c...

SUNDAES

SUPER	2.70	
JUMBO	2.00	

CRATER COPERNICUS- Devil's foo... topped with custard, hot fudge, and whipped cre...

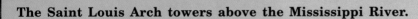

ST. LOUIS, MO

The Saint Louis Arch towers above the Mississippi River.

Dear Mom,
We went to a great custard stand. The custards are called "concretes" because they are so thick. We each got a custard and drove away. Ten minutes later, we came back for more. Then we went to see the Saint Louis Arch. It's taller than the Statue of Liberty. We took an elevator to the top. From the top of the Arch, the boats on the Mississippi River look like toys. Miss you, Pat

Mr
Pre
Chi
606

We visited President Lincoln's home.

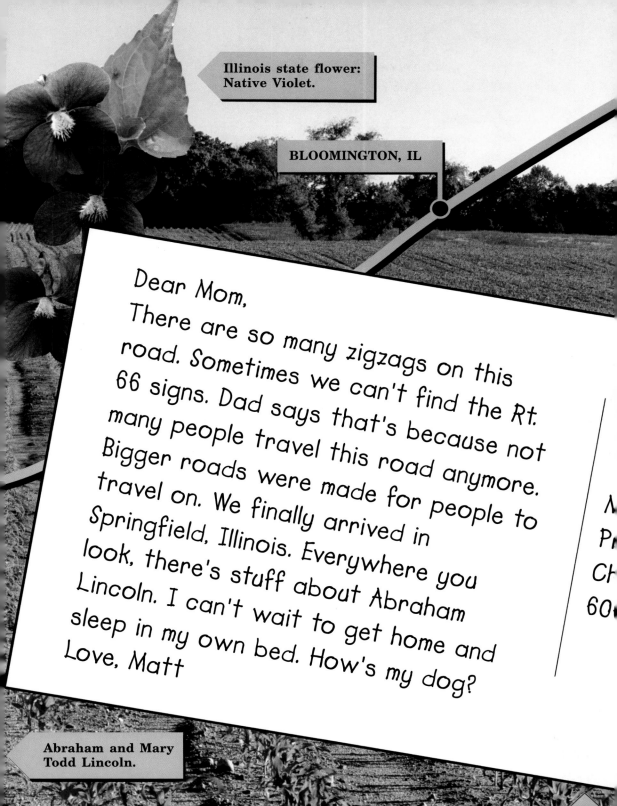

BLOOMINGTON, IL

Dear Mom,
There are so many zigzags on this road. Sometimes we can't find the Rt. 66 signs. Dad says that's because not many people travel this road anymore. Bigger roads were made for people to travel on. We finally arrived in Springfield, Illinois. Everywhere you look, there's stuff about Abraham Lincoln. I can't wait to get home and sleep in my own bed. How's my dog?
Love, Matt

M
Pr
Ch
60

Abraham and Mary Todd Lincoln.

day twelve
US 66

Miles of Route 66 per State

Miles of Road

450
400
350
300
250
200
150
100
50
0

CA AZ NM TX OK KS MO IL

State

CHICAGO

Driving Rt. 66 was a lot of fun. For two weeks, it was our road!